I0491118

Enabling Innovation:

Building a Creative
Culture in 45 Minutes

MATT D.M. WATSON, Ph.D.

DEDICATION

To my muse Jacqueline, you inspire my creativity.

CONTENTS

ACKNOWLEDGMENTS

A special thank you to my dissertation chair Martine Jago, who always pushed for greater insights. Also, to you, Mom, the creativity enabler, my father, the innovative mentor, and to my brother, Andy, the family philosopher. I had the perfect innovative environment growing up. My children, Mia and Josephine, the producers of the most creative and unique ideas, thank you for making me think deeply to understand on a different level.

CHAPTER 1
INTRODUCTION

"The value of an idea lies in the using of it."

Thomas Edison

Hostess Brands, amongst different name variations, originated in 1919. The company rapidly became and remained a staple of Americans' diet throughout the rest of the century, bringing to the public Wonder Bread, Dolly Madison Baked Goods, and the jewel of packaged desserts, the Twinkie. As a result, most houses and nearly every lunchbox in the 1970s contained a Hostess brand product. Yet, 30 years later, their company became an apparition of the past.

Hostess was never able to effectively move into the second phase of the corporate lifecycle. Because the company never introduced new products that would align with the changing customer base, their game clock started counting down. As America became more health-conscious, Hostess products were targeted as a direct contributor to the obesity epidemic. Instead of introducing a new line of health-oriented snacks to combat this threat, Hostess maintained their posture of continuing to wring every dollar out of their historic products when they should have been focusing their efforts on establishing a second life. This culture of maintenance over innovation was the first symptom of their eventual death.[1]

---

[1] *"10 Companies That Failed to Innovate and What Happened to Them,"*
June 17, 2018 [Online]. Available: https://www.vocoli.com/blog/july-
2014/10-companies-that-failed-to-innovate-and-what-happened-to-them/.

By the time of the company's demise, Hostess had over 18,500 employees, 600 distribution centers, and 36 bakeries. After navigating through a maze of bankruptcies, buyouts, and acquisitions, the company found themselves in a poor strategic position. Having 372 separate union contracts to adhere to and 5,500 overlapping delivery routes throughout the United States that were controlled by collective bargaining agreements handicapped the company.[2] Furthermore, increasing costs in gasoline, flour, and sugar, depreciating equipment, and unmanageable pension plans compounded their issues.[3]

In 2012, Hostess finally capitulated as their costs continued to overwhelm their revenue. While this is a specific example of a company faltering from a failure to innovate and reinvent themselves, it is more of a precursor to a multitude of organizations that continue to operate for the time being. This book will focus on the contribution of leadership to facilitating innovation within an organization. One requisite leadership skill of the future will be the ability to create an environment that actively encourages and enables innovative thought. As a result, this ability to facilitate

---

[2] K.J. Flanders, "Hostess brands inc.: A case study," Journal of Business and Retail Management Research, pp. 155–160, 2017.
[3] T. Ryan, "Hostess Brands – The Sweet Taste Of Success, The Bitter Bite Of Failure," June 17, 2018 [Online]. Available: http://www.gps-business.net/hostess-brands-the-sweet-taste-of-success-the-bitter-bite-of-failure/.

creativity throughout the organization will prevent the next great corporate meltdown.

Average Age of Companies

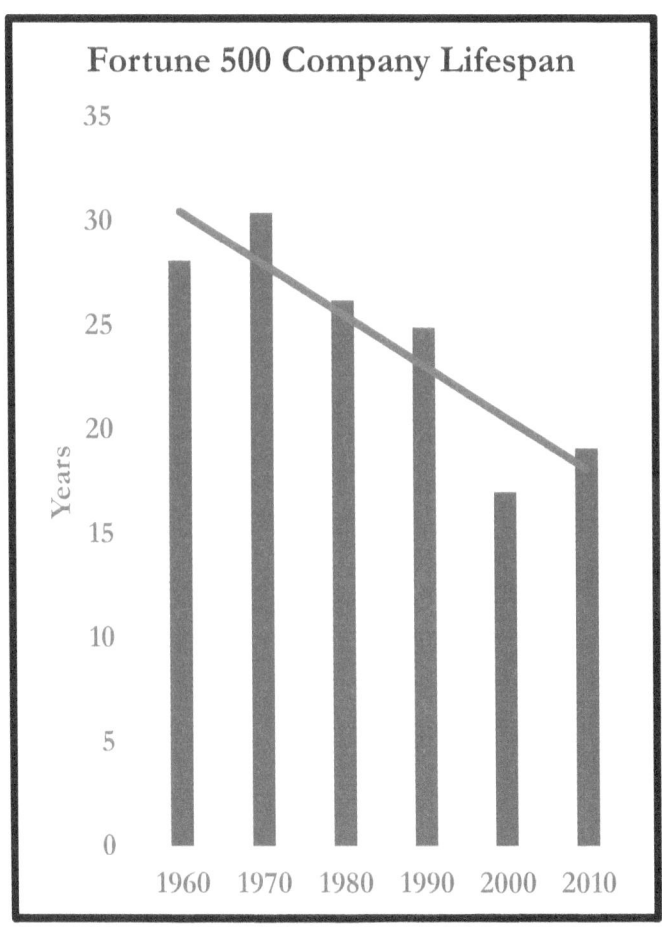

NOTES:

1. What companies do you see collapsing in the next 5 years?

_____

_____

_____

_____

2. What are the indicators that give you that impression?

_____

_____

_____

_____

3. What could they do to change those potential outcomes?

_____

_____

_____

_____

CHAPTER 2
BACKGROUND

"Innovation is the unrelenting drive to break the status quo and develop anew where few have dared to go."

Steven Jeffes

I n 2004, W. Chan Kim and Renée Mauborgne wrote about competitive marketplaces and coined the terms Red and Blue Oceans. A Red Ocean is analogous to contested markets in which there is a constant fight for dominance. However, a Blue Ocean represents an uncontested marketplace because it is newly created. Through their research, the authors demonstrated that the companies that have succeeded over the long term are the ones that have continued to prioritize the creation of new Blue Oceans instead of fighting wars of attrition while trying to maintain a grip on market share.[4]

The BlackBerry mobile smartphone is an example of achieving a Blue Ocean by pairing their cell phones with an e-mail service in 1999. For several years, they dominated the mobile market and maintained a stronghold in business sales. Eventually, the market became saturated with competitors. Instead of trying to create a new evolution, BlackBerry chose to fight to maintain their share of the market. Their corporate death followed.[5]

---

[4] *W. Chan Kim & R. Mauborgne, Blue Ocean Strategy, Boston, MA: Harvard Business Review, 2005.*

[5] *"BlackBerry timeline: A look back at the tech company's history," Global News and the Canadian Press, 24 September 2013.*

Most MBAs leading organizations will repeat these stories of failing to innovate and continue to fall into similar traps. As organizations grow and shareholders, analysts, and executives express rising expectations, leadership responds by emphasizing innovation but behaving in a way that stresses stability and repeatability. Having a desire to create a foreseeable performance leads to the development of safe evaluation models. As a result, models become predictable in nature, which leads directly to favoring incremental over disruptive initiatives. It is easier to predict incremental innovations. Empirically grounded initiatives are easier to recover from if they fail.

Both disruptive innovations and the Blue Ocean strategy fall into a different category, one of unpredictability. With the proposal of a disruptive innovation, modeling financial returns on investment and customer adoption both become unknowns. Because the data are poor, the market is yet to be defined, and the risks are significant, which leads to organizations choosing safer incremental projects. However, these incremental gains are only tactical maneuvering to win a battle in a war that will continue for years. The disruptive model is the strategic approach that views losing a handful of battles as necessary sacrifices to win the longer-term war.[6]

---

[6] C. Christensen, *The Innovator's Dilemma: When New Technologies Cause Great Firms to Fail*, Boston, MA: Harvard Business Review Press, 1997.

It is easy for an executive and management group to instruct their teams to be more creative, to bring forward disruptive ideas, and to be beacons of innovation. However, there are two specific occasions when these plans fail. The first is to start with roles built for standardization and not for innovation. For example, a pharmacist technician refilling a prescription would not want to be creative when following a standardized procedure. This would be targeting creativity to areas more apt for innovation versus providing a generalized notion to be creative.

Secondly would be to kill an idea as it is brought forward. This happens because the organization doesn't have the capability, capacity, or courage to act on those ideas. As a result, the innovator becomes dejected and loses faith in the possibility that the organization will act upon the best ideas.

R&D Risk Profile

	Continuous Improvement Projects	Low Risk & Medium Payoff Projects	High Risk & High Payoff Projects
Effort & Funding	50%	35%	15%

11

NOTES:

1. What was the last innovation that your organization delivered?

   _____
   _____
   _____
   _____

2. Did it differentiate you from your competitors?

   _____
   _____
   _____
   _____

3. What was the last great idea that you didn't implement and why?

   _____
   _____
   _____
   _____

CHAPTER 3
IMPACT

"Creativity is thinking up new ideas. Innovation is doing new things."

Theodore Levitt

A dejected creator can be a dangerous force in an organization. Successful innovators, by contrast, continue to pitch new ideas. They celebrate the one out of ten ideas accepted. In contrast, less resilient innovators typically quit trying and become silently disengaged or even shift into a passive-aggressive culture killer. From this state of mind, they use emotional stories of rejection to shape the actions of the people within their sphere of influence.

These stories turn into folklore legends that are embellished and fester in commonly heard statements:

"We've tried that before and it didn't work."

"Leadership only want you to agree with them and they are not really interested in what you have to say."

"Watch, you will put together a list of great things to do, and not a damn thing will happen."

This is how a negative culture takes root and becomes nearly impossible to resurrect. Before long, the organization will follow behaviors and ideas driven by safety and a desire to not rock the boat. Constricted by these weak ways of thinking, multiple perspectives become extinct and ideas begin to stagnate. These predictable ideas then lead to protectionism and eventual organizational death.

With their revolutionary inventory tracking system, Borders Group booksellers established a firm foothold in the publishing and retail environment. This drove such a high level of efficiency that Borders could expand significantly. In the early 1990s, the brothers Carl and Bruce Borders sold their company to Kmart, which then became independent four years later. During that time, both Barnes & Noble and Borders were growing aggressively during the dawn of the Internet. Barnes & Noble chose to develop their own ecommerce platform to sell books, while Borders chose to focus their efforts on a global expansion and decided to outsource their online book sales to a small start-up, Amazon.[7]

During this timeframe, Borders experienced significant management turnover, and their original culture of aggressive innovation had turned into passive maintenance. Another side effect of the rotating management team was that company leaders no longer had industry expertise, leaving them with a limited ability to diagnose the key issues facing their company. For one thing, the company culture was built to silence the insight of their staff members, the same staff that had the ability to diagnose the issues. For that reason, Borders was over-extended. They were slow to get on the web. They never developed an e-reader. By

[7] P. Osnos, "What Went Wrong at Borders," The Atlantic, 11 January 2011.

2011, store closings and layoffs were inevitable. Within three months, the company was insolvent, having existed as a corporation only a short 40 years.[8]

---

[8] *J. Sanburn, "5 Reasons Borders Went Out of Business," Time, 19 July 2011.*

Innovation Morale Thumbrule

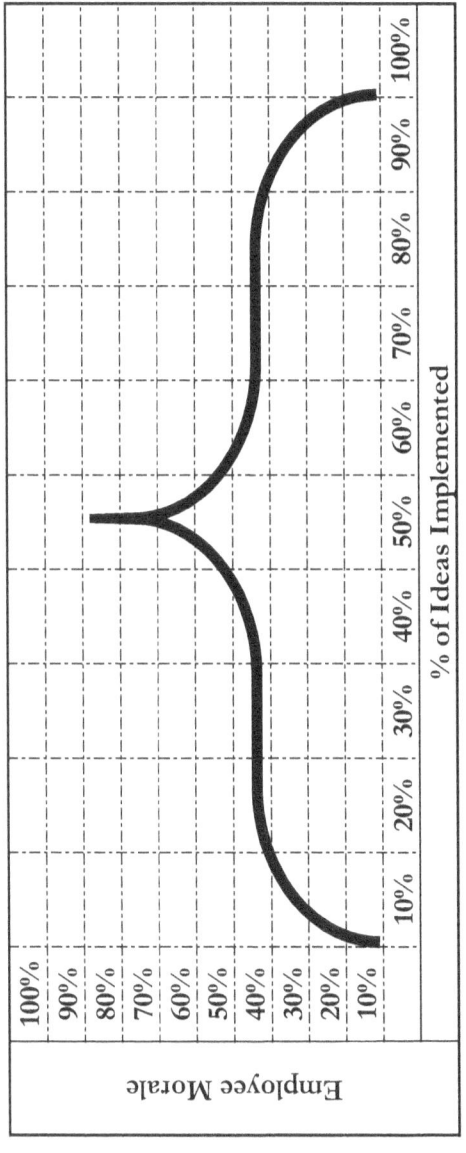

NOTES:

1. What is your organization's biggest threat?

_____

_____

_____

_____

2. How can you build creative resilience in your organization?

_____

_____

_____

_____

3. Where will the next new idea come from and when will it come?

_____

_____

_____

_____

CHAPTER 4
UNDERLYING ISSUES

"I believe you have to be willing to be misunderstood if you're going to innovate."

Jeff Bezos

At the root of this phenomenon is the fact that innovation is hard to manage. Simply put, most leadership and management practices focus on bringing clarity, order, and alignment, which runs counter-intuitive to the creative mindset. The distinguished psychologist Mihaly Csikszentmihalyi captured the traits of the creative person, noting that they are highly energetic, smart and naive, playful and disciplined, their reality is rooted in fantasy, and they are highly independent, curious, questioning, open to new ideas, and divergent thinkers.[9]

Taking those attributes and evaluating them against behavioral models that begin in school reveals a wide gap between school conformity and student creativity. Numerous studies have validated these findings that teachers show preferential treatment to students that show traits that are counter to creativity: conformity, unquestioning acceptance of authority, and compliance. The studies also point out that teachers routinely suppress creative traits and, in some cases, label creative children as obnoxious rowdies. Progressing from schooling to organizational settings, the leadership behaviors of creative suppression parallel each other.[10]

---

[9] M. Csikszentmihalyi, "The Creative Personality," Psychology Today, 1996.
[10] E.L. Westby & V.L. Dawson, "Creativity: Asset or Burden in the

A staple of solid management is sound discipline and order. Looking back on Napoleon's Army and going forward to Frederick Taylor's view on industrial management, to avoid variation is the goal. These leaders desired repeatability, standardization, and as little deviation as possible. These practices are still in place today and extend into the area of knowledge workers, whose leadership inherited the legacy of a solid management that had a firm blueprint of how their organization worked and whose managers were the central players in its operations. Maintaining that level of control, however, eliminates the usefulness of curious employees who are encouraged to question why and experiment with different ways to do the same task.

Performance reviews, bonus structures, and promotions reinforce this stifling behavior. Individuals that rock the boat the least are the ones that can be depended on. The oppression of innovation persists, boredom and stagnation set in, then disengagement and attrition follow. Those that create leave while those that adhere to process stay in the organization, comfortable with a culture that has no ability to create and disrupt the marketplace.

Fortunately, the world is experiencing a worldwide revolution of growth in complexity at an exponential rate. Some work models and processes

Classroom?", Creativity Research Journal, pp. 1–10, 1995.

change with each iteration. Work is becoming more ambiguous, with the result that it is increasingly impossible for a centralized leadership figure to control everything. This new reality is bringing forward a new kind of manager. Not a manager of a product, but a manager of complexity, one who will find famine if their focus is on control and will feast if their focus is on facilitating innovation.

Culture Diagnostic Template

Environment	Flow of Operations

Team Dynamics	Leadership

NOTES:

1. How are you discouraging innovative ideas?

   _____

   _____

   _____

   _____

2. How are you enabling innovative ideas?

   _____

   _____

   _____

   _____

3. What are some of the best practices of enabling innovation that you've seen other companies apply?

   _____

   _____

   _____

   _____

CHAPTER 5
A NEW FRAMEWORK

"If you look at history, innovation doesn't come just from giving people incentives; it comes from creating environments where their ideas can connect."

Steven Johnson

I nstead of attempting to map the architecture of how a dynamic organization operates to gain control, I propose not a different approach but a different mindset toward leading innovation. This model puts the focus on creating the optimal environment for specialized experts to succeed in managing through ambiguity in their areas of complexity. For this reason, the call is for the manager to release control and give authority to the most knowledgeable among the company's employees. This paradigm shift contains the founding cornerstones of innovation enablement. To simplify the concept of an innovation environment, imagine an organization broken into four intertwined quadrants of environment, workflow, team dynamics, and facilitative leadership.

The environment is the backbone of an organization. It drives both good and bad behaviors while also being the linchpin of how work gets accomplished. In the context of innovation, the environment holds the key to organizational encouragement or discouragement of innovation. All great innovations begin with a sound **vision,** which will provide two key facets of the creative process. First, it sets a tangible target for people to strive for, while also giving a general direction to guide them.

The second aspect is predicated on the

organization's ability to execute an idea by establishing and sharing a picture of the future with the organization, ultimately helping to align the internal resources needed to bring the idea to fruition.[11] Next, there needs to be an organizational emphasis on being able to **express ideas safely.** The creators should not feel pressured or threatened but preferably relaxed and alert. This has a direct tie to Maslow's hierarchy of needs, which postulates that before an individual can achieve peak performance, they need to have their physiological and safety needs met.[12]

Lastly, an environment is defined by the behaviors that it rewards and punishes. The key to this is not the rewarding of the outcome but the **rewarding of individuals taking risks**. Through this mechanism, individuals can take greater social risks. This will lead to more creative ideas.[13] Netflix has made painstaking efforts to skillfully craft their culture in which innovation is the necessary heartbeat. Captured within their notable culture is the employees' ability and freedom to take risks. The emphasis is if it doesn't work, fix it quickly, learn from it, and keep innovating.

If the environment is the backbone of an

---

[11] F. Hesselbein & P.M. Cohen (Eds.), Leader to leader: Enduring Insights on Leadership from the Drucker Foundation's Award-Winning Journal, San Francisco: Jossey-Bass, 1999.
[12] M.I. Stein, Stimulating Creativity, New York: Academic Press, 1974.
[13] A.H. Maslow, Motivation and Personality, New York: Harper & Row, 1987.

organization, then the flow of operations is the circulatory system that keeps the body moving. The Lean methodology looks at this organizational flow searching for constraints to the flow pattern to improve efficiency and effectiveness, and the same can be said of the flow of innovation. When designing an office work model or a timebound workshop, an important factor is to ensure a smooth flow of ideas that don't become constrained. This creates the facilitation of **more ideas** or a mass of ideas, which in turn has a direct correlation to better ideas where quantity breeds quality. This falls into the situation where individuals start their idea processes with the easy solutions or ideas that are close to the top of their mind; the more ideas they must produce, the greater the depth of creativity they will be forced to explore.[14]

The second aspect is that while innovation is noted for being optimal as an individual experience, the outcomes can be parochial in nature. The genesis of group collaboration includes the infusion of **multiple perspectives**. By applying a variety of inputs, ideas can take a different form and address solutions with greater assurances of achieving customer satisfaction.[15] While this can create the opportunity to impede the flow of

---

[14] *M.I. Stein, Stimulating Creativity, New York: Academic Press, 1974.*
[15] *M. West, "Innovation Implementation in Work Teams," in Group Creativity, Innovation Through Collaboration, Oxford, UK, Oxford University Press, 2003, pp. 245–276.*

ideas, it will also build the opportunity for the team to combine and scaffold their ideas together resulting in a higher quality of ideas.

The final aspect is creating the process allowing your team to go into **deep and focused thought**. Typically, office work consists of busy and shallow work; this is the work that can be done with distractions and via multitasking. Deep work is the kind of mentally all-encompassing effort that ultimately challenges the team to stretch to new heights; this is where ideas are born. Deep thought is an absolute for creativity; it is necessary to eliminate added interference so that individuals may be able to achieve a greater level of deep thought, ultimately inducing innovation.[16]

The director of *Dunkirk* and *The Dark Knight Trilogy* movies, Christopher Nolan, emphasizes these points by banning phones on his movie sets, inspired by the belief that there are bubbles of creativity in which people will get lost in engaged, creative thought. The main culprit of bursting those bubbles is the distraction created by phones, yanking people out of their deep level of concentration.

As noted earlier in this book and throughout

---

[16] *M. Csikszentmihalyi, "The Creative Personality," Psychology Today, 1996.*

the body of research, a single individual produces greater innovation than a group of people. There are several causes of this, from the phenomenon of groupthink and a lack of safety in sharing ideas to failing to incorporate all the perspectives and having an overly dominant opinion take over the group. However, with this being known, a team of innovators still has the potential to create powerful ideas if they are guided correctly. Distinct from individual innovations, team creations allow for the building of multiple perspectives off the participants' expertise, increasing the chances of the solution addressing the issue and adopting one overall idea. The key to achieving this state is refining your team dynamics to enable this level of innovation. This starts with **balanced team participation** and not letting one person dominate the discussion, as this will negatively impact the ability to gain the participation of all attendees.[17]

Secondly, there is a need to create a team environment whose participants are **playful, trusting, and vulnerable**. Ensuring a safe environment for sharing ideas elicits the most ideas from people. Associated with vulnerability is the team's level of playfulness. Their willingness to have fun with one another is the key to creating a joyful environment.

[17] *C.J. Nemeth & B. Nemeth-Brown, "Better Than Individuals?", in Group Creativity: Innovation Through Collaboration, Oxford, UK, Oxford University Press, 2003, pp. 63–84.*

Similarly, in such an environment, not only are people comfortable with their teammates but happy to be with them.[18]

Lastly, a leader will want to create a team that is **cognitively diverse and comfortable debating** among themselves. Creativity is improved by incorporating the ideas of people with different technical specialties and cognitive thought processes. Cognitive diversity, or different ways of thinking, provides the conditions for convergent and divergent thought. Having a diversity of backgrounds enables a range of individual cultures within the team, creating opportunities for cognitive diversity. This will also elicit debate and argument in the group to challenge the merits of ideas and ensure a full perspective is taken.[19]

One of the main concerns with group or team brainstorming is the prevalence of groupthink. This phenomenon negatively impacts effectiveness, as the goal shifts from creating originality to achieving consensus. One of the main issues of achieving a majority view is that people naturally gravitate toward consensus, even if it is the wrong decision or choice.

---

[18] M. Watson, *Common Strategies and Practices Among Facilitators of Innovative Thinking in Organizations*, Ann Arbor, MI: ProQuest, 2018.
[19] F.J. Milliken, C.A. Bartel, & T.R. Kurtzberg, "Diversity and Creativity in Work Groups," in P.B. Paulus & B.A. Nijstad (Eds.), *Group Creativity, Innovation Through Collaboration*, Oxford, UK, Oxford University Press, 2003, pp. 32–62.

Research has found that the application of friction, debate, and dissent stimulates the thought process to help achieve multiple perspectives on an issue. The goal of a team should be achieving candid discussions.[20] Wilbur and Orville Wright had the advantage of being brothers but maximized this approach. During the building of the first airplane, the brothers believed that they thought as one. However, it was common for them to fight and debate for weeks over pivotal decisions.

Leadership is many things to many people, and as for innovation, it is the culmination of creative success. Encouraging leadership can inspire just as quickly as pessimistic leadership can mute innovative initiatives. The key to success is focusing first on a leader who **awards autonomy and then lets the process unfold free of judgment**. Being innovative and creating something out of nothing is a masterful art and one in which a person needs to have the autonomy to experiment and explore on their track toward mastery. This mental activation can manifest in many forms, ranging from walking and taking naps to playing video games and doodling.

As the creator refines their process of innovation, it is key for the facilitative leader to

---

[20] B. Hennessey, "Is the Social Psychology of Creativity Really Social?," in P.B. Paulus & B.A. Nijstad (Eds.), Group Creativity, Innovation Through Collaboration, Oxford, Oxford University Press, 2003, pp. 181–201.

encourage this behavior. This is in contrast to fixating on any abnormal deviations from the norm. Being able to **release control to explore ambiguity** enables the creator to delve into their deep and focused work. The shallow work that resides in the structured norms of an organization results in benchmarking competitors and maintaining the status quo. The deep work that explores ambiguous relationships, social connections, and complexities leads to market-shifting disruptive innovations.

This brings us to the last essential emphasis, which is to **encourage creativity and be patient enough to let it develop**. Not every gamble will pay off and neither will every initiative. Venture capitalists bet on ten companies with the expectation that only one will achieve greatness.[21] The company that achieves greatness covers the wagers placed on the organizations that don't come to fruition.

The multinational pharmaceutical company Pfizer went through this same process in the early 1990s, while on a quest to create high blood pressure and chest pain medication. As the trials proved unsuccessful, the product came close to being shelved. Fortunately, the researchers found that the substance could address erectile dysfunction. This patience

---

[21] *M. Watson, Common Strategies and Practices Among Facilitators of Innovative Thinking in Organizations, Ann Arbor, MI: ProQuest, 2018.*

played out, resulting in a dramatic market shift from the original vision, leading to a twenty-year, $32 billion-dollar revenue run for Viagra. While the intent was specific in the beginning, the innovation cycle is never a straight path, nor does it ever end exactly as perceived. Maintaining patience to see the outcome can pay huge dividends in the end.

Facilitating Innovation Best Practices

Environment	Flow of Operations
Vision	Quantity of Ideas
Safety in Sharing Ideas	Applying Multiple Perspectives
Rewarding Risk Taking	Deep & Focused Work
Team Dynamics	**Leadership**
Balanced Participation	Autonomy & Judgement Free
Team That Is Playful, Trusting & Vulnerable	Creativity Encouragement & Patience
Cognitive Diversity & Candid Debaters	Releasing Control & Exploring Ambiguity

NOTES:

1. Describe your organization's work environment.

    _____

    _____

    _____

2. Describe your organization's workflow.

    _____

    _____

    _____

3. Describe your organization's team dynamics.

    _____

    _____

    _____

4. Describe your organization's leadership.

    _____

    _____

    _____

CHAPTER 6
IMPLEMENTATION

"The secret of change is to focus all of your energy, not on fighting the old, but on building the new."

Socrates

T ips and insights on how to be more innovative are interesting and anecdotal. They are also difficult to put into action that leads to behavior change. Therefore, the priority is to understand what the impediments to being creative are and how to implement cultures that can act disruptively. Linking awareness to change can be a powerful approach to awakening an individual to their reality.

When asked by a client how innovative their culture is, the typical response is to err on the side of positivity. In such cases, company representatives insist that they are more innovative than most and attempt to make a direct link to how their culture is the cause. Using quantitative surveys, qualitative focus groups, and observations, an independent assessor can accurately triangulate a picture of an organizational culture. This helps determine how well the leader's assessment aligns with the teams. This also creates an understanding of where a team can be innovative and where a team must be process-driven and standardized.

Assessment is a valuable component of changing behaviors. My mother's philosophy that "people don't change after kindergarten" runs counter to this approach. However, it accurately captures the understanding that behavioral change is one of the hardest tasks an organization can undertake. Many clients will look at the number of weaknesses pointed out and will disregard everything and do nothing. Other clients will go the other extreme by building a massive corrective action plan in an attempt to solve everything. These gyrations both end with the same result of no progress accomplished.

A healthier approach would be to follow the guidance of Richard Thaler's Nudge Theory. The theory focuses on small, incremental, and almost unnoticeable changes. These nudge people in the direction of making a better decision. For example, to encourage healthier eating, Nudge Theory would suggest placing fruit or vegetables at eye level, near the checkout counter of the grocery store instead of displaying candy bars.[22] Using this same approach, as a team, choose one behavior or cultural aspect to change. Then, design how each team member can be nudged into the behavior that would help enable innovative thinking. Make this one behavior the focus of the team for the next few weeks. Practice feedback on performance with each other to get it to stick and, after six weeks, if the behavior has changed, then move

---

[22] C. Sunstein & R. Thaler, Nudge: Improving Decisions about Health, Wealth, and Happiness, New Haven, CN: Yale University Press, 2008.

to the next area of weakness.

This approach came to life when consulting with a manufacturing organization whose executive staff kept focusing on tactics and operations. This led to a stagnant business model. With phones, messages, and interruptions constantly occurring, the team was never able to achieve a level of deep and focused effort, nor were they able to define a long-term growth strategy. Adopting a Nudge process, they were able to build a two-hour block of time at the end of each day. There they established expectations enabling them to shut off their phones, close their e-mails, and decline meetings so that they could dedicate their efforts to building a long-term strategy. While this was intended to be a short-term resolution to build a strategy, it soon became ingrained within the culture of the organization with the time blocks moving to the management and engineer levels.

Lastly, try to build a comprehensive working prototype as a group that can take your team through a simple project. The idea is that you will be able to define your creative process and begin preparing to handle greater levels of ambiguity. Choose a safe project to practice on, design, and build a flow of operations for the project with a specific focus on how the project can be run with the greatest inspiration of creativity. This will provide the opportunity to understand the team's preferences for how they will be able to unlock their reserved insights as well as establish behavioral guidelines to operate with. This experience will help the team explore the pros and cons of the model with the intent of designing a future operating model that will unlock innovation during the projects that matter most.

Innovation Assessment Model

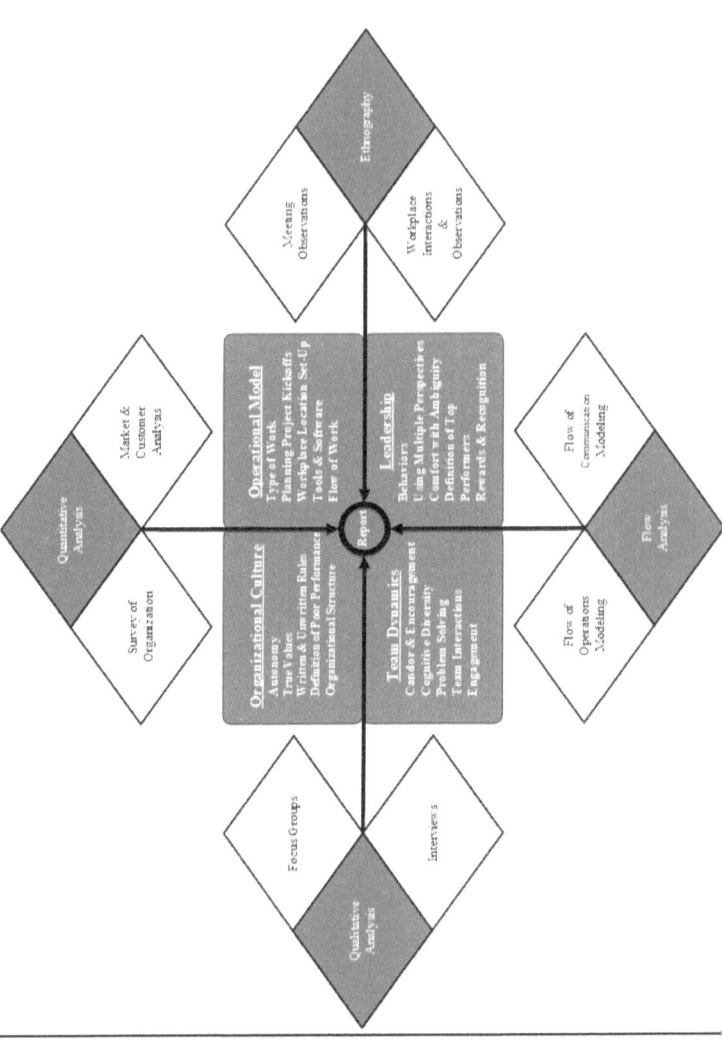

NOTES:

1. How creative is your organization and why?

   _____
   _____
   _____
   _____

2. What behaviors do you need to change in order to enable greater creativity?

   _____
   _____
   _____
   _____

3. How can you change your behaviors?

   _____
   _____
   _____
   _____

REFERENCES

[1] "10 Companies That Failed to Innovate and What Happened to Them," 17 June 2018 [Online]. Available: https://www.vocoli.com/blog/july-2014/10-companies-that-failed-to-innovate-and-what-happened-to-them/.

[2] K.J. Flanders, "Hostess brands inc.: A case study," *Journal of Business and Retail Management Research,* pp. 155–160, 2017.

[3] T. Ryan, "Hostess Brands – The Sweet Taste Of Success, The Bitter Bite Of Failure," 17 June 2018 [Online]. Available: http://www.gps-business.net/hostess-brands-the-sweet-taste-of-success-the-bitter-bite-of-failure/.

[4] W. Chan Kim & Renée Mauborgne, *Blue Ocean Strategy*, Boston, MA: Harvard Business Review, 2005.

[5] "BlackBerry timeline: A look back at the tech company's history," *Global News and the Canadian Press,* 24 September 2013.

[6] C. Christensen, *The Innovator's Dilemma: When New Technologies Cause Great Firms to Fail*, Boston, MA: Harvard Business Review Press, 1997.

[7] P. Osnos, "What Went Wrong at Borders," *The Atlantic,* 11 January 2011.

[8] J. Sanburn, "5 Reasons Borders Went Out of Business," *Time,* 19 July 2011.

[9] M. Csikszentmihalyi, "The Creative Personality," *Psychology Today,* 1996.

[10] E. L. Westby &. V. L. Dawson, "Creativity: Asset or Burden in the Classroom?", *Creativity Research Journal,* pp. 1–10, 1995.

[11] F. Hesselbein & P. M. Cohen, Leader to leader: Enduring insights on leadership from the Drucker Foundation's award-winning journal, San Francisco: Jossey-Bass, 1999.

[12] M. I. Stein, *Stimulating Creativity*, New York: Academic Press, 1974.

[13] F. R. Maslow, *Motivation and Personality*, New York: Harper and Row, 1987.

[14] M. West, "Innovation Implementation in Work Teams," in *Group Creativity, Innovation Through Collaboration*, Oxford, UK, Oxford University Press, 2003, pp. 245–276.

[15] C. J. Nemeth & B. Nemeth-Brown, "Better Than Individuals?", in *Group Creativity, Innovation Through Collaboration*, Oxford, UK, Oxford University Press, 2003, pp. 63–84.

[16] M. Watson, *Common Strategies and Practices Among Facilitators of Innovative Thinking in Organizations*, Ann Arbor, MI: ProQuest, 2018.

[17] F. J. Milliken, C. A. Bartel, & T. R. Kurtzberg, "Diversity and Creativity in Work Groups," in P. B. Paulus & B. A. Nijstad (Eds.), *Group Creativity, Innovation Through Collaboration*, Oxford, UK, Oxford University Press, 2003, pp. 32–62.

[18] B. Hennessey, "Is the Social Psychology of Creativity Really Social?," in *Group Creativity,*

Innovation Through Collaboration, Oxford, Oxford University Press, 2003, pp. 181–201.

[19] R. H. &. S. C. R. Thaler, *Nudge: Improving decisions about Health, Wealth, and Happiness*, New Haven, CN: Yale University Press, 2008.

9M CONSULTING

About 9m Consulting

9m Consulting helps enable innovation for businesses that are navigating transformation. Unlike other firms, we specialize in building a creative culture that can pivot.

Our Approach

9m is a firm dedicated to guiding organizations through large-scale transitions. Our approach is to work with our clients to understand their issues, opportunities, and perspectives. Instead of applying a one-size-fits-all approach, we apply 9m's agile innovation model. This is more than a process but a framework that provides the right solution to the right problem.

➢ Beginning with culture, 9m diagnoses the current environment and impediments to innovation.
➢ This leads to the next focus area of leadership development and team dynamics. We prime the teams for group innovation through development and creativity training.
➢ Next, we provide customized, facilitated events that enable creative pinnacles. These events range from strategic planning and business development to problem-solving and product development.

➤ With creation comes disruption. 9m is able to shift its attention to change management planning. We guide clients through a change simulation model to transition the organization expertly. Next, we guide the strategy selection and implementation planning.

<u>9m Approach</u>

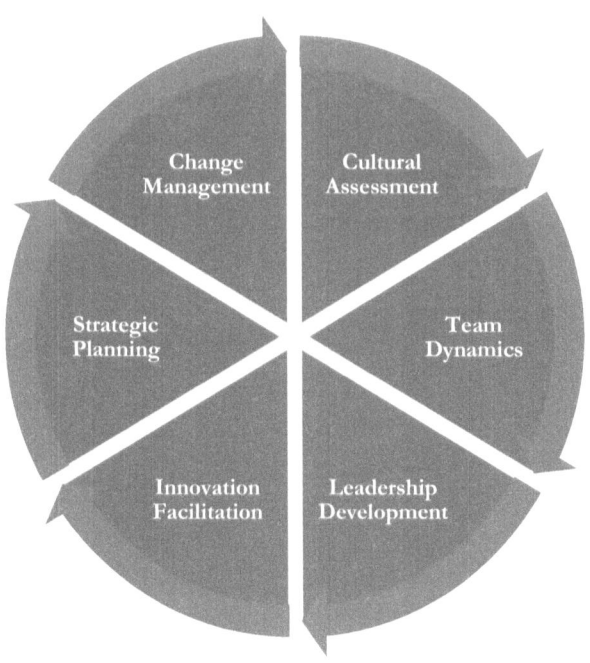

ABOUT THE AUTHOR

Author and Principal Consultant

Matt D.M. Watson, Ph.D., PMP, is the founder and Principal of 9m, an innovation consulting firm based in Boise, Idaho. He began his career in the United States Air Force as a forward-air-controller, serving in the invasion of Iraq with the 101st Airborne Division. Following Matt's service, he worked with the Bechtel Corporation as an organizational development project manager and training director. Later he worked with Hewlett-Packard as a business strategy project manager and is the Chairman of the Board for the Community Veterans Justice Project.

He obtained his Bachelor of Arts in Organizational Leadership from Chapman University and Master of Arts in Learning Technologies from Pepperdine University. After spending the first half of his career specializing in organizational development, project management, and lean process improvements, Matt focused his craft on the creative and innovation processes while completing his Ph.D. in Global Leadership and Change at Pepperdine University. There he was able to refine his innovation model while completing his research on the enablement of creativity.

He is the author of the following:

- ➤ Corporate Musings During the Pandemic
- ➤ The Workplace Olympian
- ➤ Strategy for the Small Business
- ➤ The Strategy Pocketbook: Building a Strategy for Tomorrow's Organization
- ➤ Nudge Change Management: Moving Organizations with Data and Transparency
- ➤ Rethinking Change Management with Nudges: Transforming Organizations in 45 Minutes
- ➤ Facilitating Innovation: Unlocking Moonshots
- ➤ Enabling Innovation: Building a Creative Culture in 45 Minutes
- ➤ The Leadership That Facilitates Innovation
- ➤ From Global Vision to Agile Execution: A Proposed Planning Model
- ➤ Simulating the Corporate Reorganization
- ➤ Common Strategies and Practices Among Facilitators of Innovative Thinking in Organizations
- ➤ Fear and Loathing in the Accountable Culture

www.ingramcontent.com/pod-product-compliance
Lightning Source LLC
Chambersburg PA
CBHW030524220526
45463CB00007B/2716